CLIMATE CHANGE

Cyclones

By Ashley McIvor

We respect and honour Aboriginal and Torres Strait Islander Elders past, present and future. We acknowledge the stories, traditions and living cultures of Aboriginal and Torres Strait Islander peoples on this land and commit to building a brighter future together.

Library For All Ltd.

Understanding Cyclones

What is a Cyclone?

Cyclones are powerful storms that form over warm tropical waters, driven by hot, humid weather conditions. The hot air rising sucks in more air, which builds into a spiral of clouds and rain.

If the weather turns calm and quiet during a cyclone, you're in the 'eye' of the storm.

A cyclone can reach up to 290 km/h wind speed.

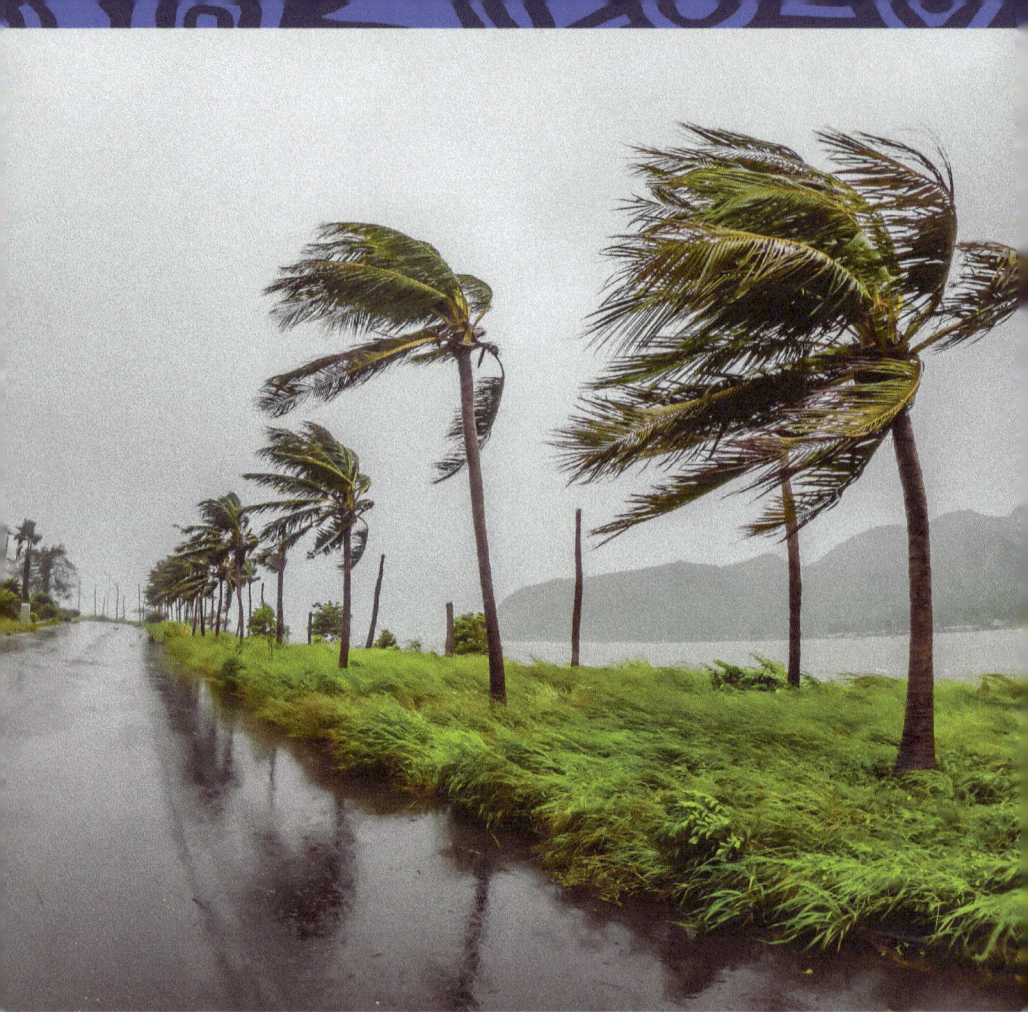

Heavy rain, strong winds, and lightning can indicate a cyclone in the area. However, you can sometimes predict a cyclone even before the storm begins! Signs of dangerous weather can be seen in nature.

Ants moving to higher ground, Grevillea plants turning yellow and flowering white, frogs croaking for a long time, and storm birds in the sky can all be indicators of oncoming cyclonic weather.

5

Preparation Strategies

The Melsonby community prepares for cyclones by moving to higher ground and using ancient rock shelters to hide from dangerous weather. They use the traditional signs from nature to tell when to start preparing for a cyclone.

Keep emergency clothes, medicine, and food up high!

Indoors is the safest place to be during a cyclone. Cyclones are usually accompanied by floods, so during your preparation, try and find somewhere dry and above ground. Develop evacuation strategies, communicate with your community, and pack essentials to take with you.

DID YOU KNOW?

You can use traditional signals, like smoke and blowing into conch shells, to communication warnings to the rest of the community.

Preparation Strategies

There are some Melsonby community practices performed when a cyclone is forecasted. Certain plants are burned to ward off heavy rain, and stories are shared with children to teach them about surviving dangerous weather.

Evacuation is also an option. If a town is in the path of a cyclone, citizens are urged to pack emergency food, blankets, medicine, important documents, then fill up their cars and head inland.

Effects on Land and Community

Cyclones bring heavy rain and often trigger other natural disasters, like floods and landslides. All these cause silt and sand to fill up rivers, damaging fish populations and available clean water.

Vegetation and land animals aren't spared, either. Habitats are flooded, and plants are destroyed by fast-flowing water, lightning, and landslides. However, many animals can sense such weather and find safety.

Losing homes, important possessions, and sometimes lives is devastating. It's important to be resilient and stay hopeful during disasters.

DID YOU KNOW?

Cyclones can destroy areas up to 1000km away from their path!

Coral reefs are vulnerable to cyclone damage and take up to a decade to regrow.

Cyclone damage happens on different timescales: short-term damage and long-term damage.

Scientific Insight on Cyclones

There are 5 categories of cyclones and they're ranked depending on their wind speed. Under 100 kilometres per hour is a category 1, while over 200 kilometres per hour is a category 5. Category 5 cyclones are the most destructive and can rip roofs off houses, destroy entire landscapes, and cause significant long-term damage to communities and environments.

CATEGORY	WIND GUST (km/h)	EFFECTS
1	90-125	
2	125-164	
3	165-224	
4	225-279	
5	280 +	

SEVERE { 3, 4, 5

* Adapted from the Bureau of Meteorology's Tropical Cyclone Category system.

Additional disasters like flooding and storms are consequences of cyclones and have a similar level of negative impact. Flooding degrades soil quality and can destroy crops, leading to long-term food shortages. These disasters are exacerbated by the speed a cyclone moves over land. The slower it is, the more intense the damages.

Response and Recovery

Immediate response to a cyclone is establishing emergency shelters on higher ground.

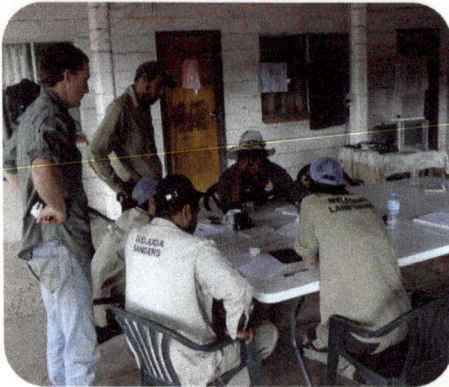

CYCLONE & EMERGENCY WELFARE CENTRE ⬆

Afterwards, Ranger groups collaborate to assist each other's communities in recovering.

Strong community spirit and collaboration is crucial to recovering from a disaster. Structural and environmental damage, along with food, water, and shelter shortages, can cause severe rifts within a community after a cyclone.

It's important to stay strong and rely on others in the aftermath.

Emergency services are critical and should be contacted as soon as possible.

Cultural Impacts and Stories

It's not just community spirit that suffers during a disaster. Cultural sites like the rock art and Bora Grounds in Melsonby are also threatened by cyclones and subsequent floods. Important parts of cultural heritage must be rebuilt, and smoking ceremonies performed to clear negative energy.

Rock art, scar trees, and cave paintings are at risk.

Vulnerable cultural sites in Melsonby

1

Scar trees can be ruined by rain and wind.

2

Rock art can be washed away or destroyed.

3

Bora grounds can be destroyed in landslides and floods.

Enhanced communication between Rangers builds resilience against future cyclones.

Community and Environmental Resilience

Strengthening community spirit also means sharing knowledge with the future generations. Children needs to know how to handle disasters themselves, especially as their frequency increases due to climate change. Storytelling is crucial when educating people about disaster survival.

How to see natural warnings needs to be passed down within community.

Photo Credits

Page	Attribution
Cover	Stocktrek Images, Inc. / Alamy Stock Photo
Pages 2-3	petesphotography/iStockphoto.com
Page 4	Elizaveta Galitckaia/Shutterstock.com
Page 5	Balash Mirzayev / Alamy Stock Photo
Page 6	Photo courtesy of the Queensland Indigenous Land and Sea Ranger Program.
Page 7	Giuseppe_R/Shutterstock.com
Pages 8–9	Photo courtesy of the Queensland Indigenous Land and Sea Ranger Program.
Page 10 (above)	Silken Photography/Shutterstock.com
Page 10 (below)	Public Domain/Pexels.com
Page 11	Daria Nipot/Shutterstock.com
Page 12	Adapted from the Bureau of Meteorology's Tropical Cyclone Category system.
Page 13	Suzanne Long / Alamy Stock Photo
Page 14 (above)	ChameleonsEye/Shutterstock.com
Page 14 (below)	Photo courtesy of the Queensland Indigenous Land and Sea Ranger Program.
Page 15	© Library For All
Page 16	Photo courtesy of the Queensland Indigenous Land and Sea Ranger Program.
Page 18 (both)	Photo courtesy of the Queensland Indigenous Land and Sea Ranger Program.
Page 19	© Library For All

You can use these questions to talk about this book with your family, friends and teachers.

What did you learn from this book?

Describe this book in one word. Funny? Scary? Colourful? Interesting?

How did this book make you feel when you finished reading it?

What was your favourite part of this book?

Queensland Indigenous Land and Sea Ranger Program

The Queensland Indigenous Land and Sea Ranger Program collaborates with First Nations communities to protect and care for land and sea Country. With over 200 rangers, the program shares cultural knowledge, engages in community education, and leads youth programs like the Junior Ranger initiative, fostering a strong connection to Country and Culture.

Ashley McIvor is a Balnggarrawarra Ranger from the Melsonby community.

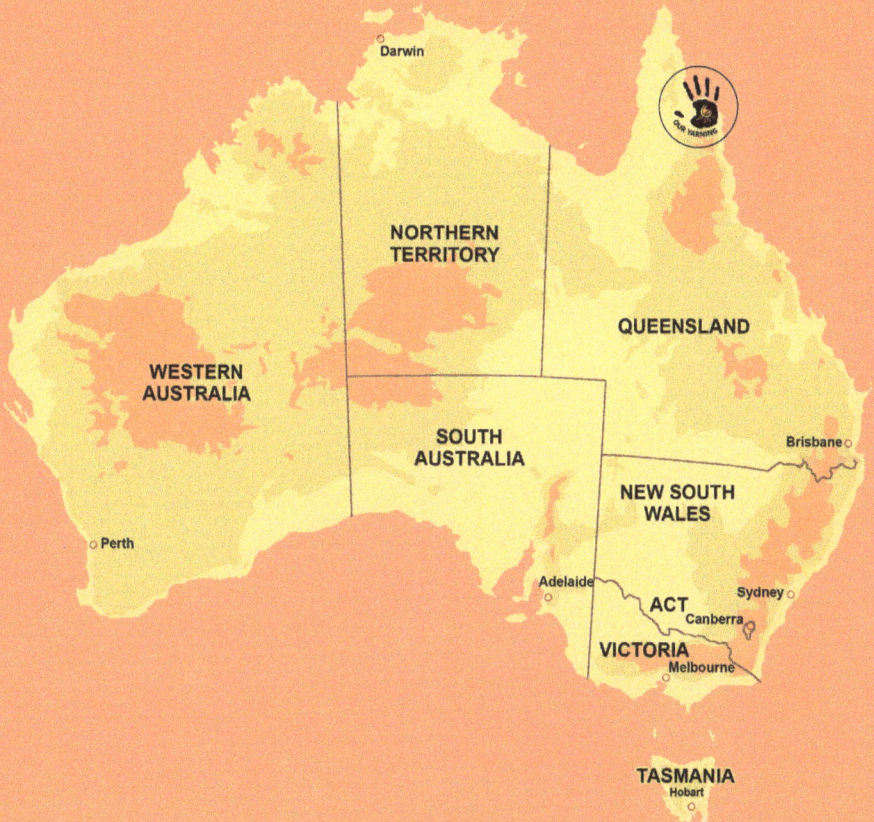

Darwin

NORTHERN TERRITORY

QUEENSLAND

WESTERN AUSTRALIA

SOUTH AUSTRALIA

Brisbane

NEW SOUTH WALES

Perth

Adelaide

Sydney

ACT
Canberra

VICTORIA
Melbourne

TASMANIA
Hobart

Our Yarning

The Our Yarning collection aligns with the Australian Curriculum through the Cross-Curriculum Priorities — Aboriginal and Torres Strait Islander Histories and Cultures. The collection provides an authentic opportunity for learning and embedding Aboriginal and Torres Strait Islander perspectives because it is written by Aboriginal and Torres Strait Islander people.

We know that children learn better, and enjoy reading more, when they see themselves in the stories, characters and illustrations of the books they read.

To download the app, visit the Google Play Store or Apple Store and search 'Our Yarning'.

libraryforall.org

You're reading Upper Primary

Learner – Beginner readers

Start your reading journey with short words, big ideas and plenty of pictures.

Level 1 – Rising readers

Raise your reading level with more words, simple sentences and exciting images.

Level 2 – Eager readers

Enjoy your reading time with familiar words, but complex sentences.

Level 3 – Progressing readers

Develop your reading skills with creative stories and some challenging vocabulary.

Level 4 – Fluent readers

Step up your reading skills with playful narratives, new words and fun facts.

Middle Primary – Curious readers

Discover your world through science and stories.

Upper Primary – Adventurous readers

Explore your world through science and stories.

DIGITAL EDUCATION
LIBRARY FOR ALL
FOR THE WORLD

Library For All is an Australian not for profit organisation with a mission to make knowledge accessible to all via an innovative digital library solution.
Visit us at libraryforall.org

Climate Change: Cyclones

First published 2024

Published by Library For All Ltd
Email: info@libraryforall.org
URL: libraryforall.org

This project was delivered with the support of QBE under the Community Ready partnership.

Community Ready

This book was made possible with the support of the Queensland Indigenous Land and Sea Ranger Program to support educational outcomes for children in Australia by learning from Indigenous knowledge and stewardship of Country. To learn more, visit https://www.qld.gov.au/environment/plants-animals/conservation/community/land-sea-rangers/locations.

Queensland Indigenous Land and Sea Rangers

Queensland Government

Our Yarning logo design by Jason Lee, Bidjipidji Art

Climate Change: Cyclones
McIvor, Ashley
ISBN: 978-1-923207-47-9
SKU04433